Cognitive Behavioral Therapy Techniques

How to Manage Anxiety and Depression Using CBT – Control Your Thinking, Emotions, and Behavior

Erika Robinson

Table of Contents

Introduction

Cognitive behavioral therapy (CBT) is a psychotherapy technique based on the identification of negative forms of behavior and thoughts, and intently the usage of stimulating techniques to restructure such behavioral and thought patterns.

CBT is basically used to deal with depression and anxiety. It protects the overwhelming effects of negative thoughts and therefore introduces the most effective coping mechanisms. CBT is most effective in dealing with school or work stress, where patients are trained to work effectively in their workspace. Cognitive behavioral therapy helps individuals to regain control of overwhelming situations and become fully functional and effective in their workspace.

You will begin to manage fears effectively. Your quality of life will improve. And you will begin to function efficiently in your personal and professional relationship. CBT is different from psychoanalysis. Psychoanalysis focuses on the recognition of reactions and motivation based on behavioral analysis. CBT, on the other hand, creates a pattern to provide a change in thought and behavioral process. CBT is the most effective therapy in dealing with thought disorders.

Cognitive behavioral therapy is action-oriented psychotherapy introducing counter-actions against negative thoughts and reactions. Restructuring negative patterns have been easier with the introduction of CBT in the 1960s by Dr. Aaron Beck.

The significance of cognitive behavioral therapy

CBT is used to deal with anxiety and depression by finding ways to shake the root cause. Apart from the physical causes of anxiety and depression, thinking patterns are also responsible for triggering the feeling of distress. CBT is focused on controlling and restructuring such thought patterns.

The following are the disorders that can be corrected by the use of cognitive behavioral therapy:

Anger problems

Low self-esteem

Eating disorder

Chronic pain

Relationship issues

Drug abuse

Alcohol abuse

Anxiety disorders

Depression

Even though the effective method of cognitive behavioral therapy is personalized based on diagnosis, outlines are almost the same. The effectiveness of the treatment is entirely dependent on the effort and willingness of the patient to carry out a series of instructions.

It all comes down to the effectiveness of the treatment based on acceptance by the individual.

CBT is all about the identification of causal thoughts of depression, panic attacks or anxiety. For example, if an individual is having a panic attack in an office, we try as much as possible to help that person recognize the thought patterns that are causing the anxiety. We first observe closely the physical symptoms, through which we can identify the most contributory thought process of such panic attacks. We work together with the patient, so they can consciously recognize such negative thinking patterns. Once the source negative thinking patterns are understood, we use cognitive behavioral therapy to control and reverse them.

We allow the individual to calm down, to an extent they can be able to think rationally. Firstly, we ask the individual how they feel before the panic attack. We tend to identify the environmental causes, as well as the mental causes. We also ask about the patient's history; whether they have experienced such attacks before—in the same environment or similar. We also ask whether anything unique has happened to trigger such attacks.

The past experiences of the individual will reveal realistic possibilities of the causes of such thinking, as well as potential processes towards avoidance. This will provide room for us to suggest an alternative thought process, or more often, to provide accurate twin-situations that will correlate two thought processes—one for the negative and the second for a new thought process to deal with the negative thought.

You have to keep in mind that anxiety causes panic attacks, but there are more effects of anxiety that are labeled as cognitive or behavioral disorders in the medical world. Being afraid is basically caused by anxiety, and most people don't realize that fears are treatable. Anxiety associated fears such as the fear of going to the movies, fear of social gatherings, fear of new buildings, fear of taking the subway, or the fear to leave the house, can be treated using simple cognitive behavioral therapy techniques. All these fears when recognized can be used to set goals using CBT for total recovery.

We focus on instructional goals. The goals are designed uniquely based on what the person wants. For example, if the individual's wish is to attend concerts and they are afraid of social gatherings, we construct a step-by-step instruction that will help the individual achieve this goal.

The first step is usually less challenging and harmless to their fear emotion. We allow the patient to slowly go up the ladder as they become familiar with the initial steps. The aim is to gain comfort and to improve on a daily basis. Individuals are not advised to move to the next step until they are comfortable with the current one.

We also keep track of distress as individuals go up the ladder. We rate each level of discomfort on the scale of 1 -10 to ascertain the exact amount of time the individual needs to spend at the particular stage before they gain comfort, and then move to the next. Since CBT is a permanent solution to get rid of fears and solve thinking disorders, we tend to move through the stages as slowly as possible, all based on the individual's response at each stage. The lower the distress level, the higher the comfort level.

Once we treat the first anxiety using such a process, we will know whether the individual has other fears or anxiety that needs to be treated or not. Once the patient adopts the skill, they can independently deal with fears and will be eager to try new things, even things that scare them.

Another aim of CBT is building the patient's confidence. Once confidence is built, they become motivated to set new goals and go the extra mile in dealing with fears.

The aim for the use of cognitive behavioral therapy is to push anxiety and depression into remission. Staying above fears and the root causes of negative thoughts will become easy.

We all go through stress in life. So, CBT is a universal technique for dealing with stress, even before it affects the nervous system. Generally, CBT takes only a few weeks to adapt and manifest effect on the patient.

People who undergo CBT at different levels tend to have more control over their emotions, stress levels and ultimately tend to be more productive when it comes to facing fears and dealing with general day-to-day challenges. We give meaning to events through our thought process. CBT focuses on the way you think and act.

The transformation of thoughts always brings immediate positive action, therefore leading to a positive response of the nervous system. The positive actions have to be productive to counter any negative thoughts or behavior.

Automatic Negative Thoughts

Automatic negative thoughts are thoughts that lead to emotional difficulties. These thought patterns lead to anxiety and depression and only recognized when the symptoms become severe. CBT is aimed at controlling those emotional difficulties caused by automatic negative thoughts. The thoughts are being examined together with the response, and then rational steps are put in place to provide evidence to refute the effect of these thoughts. This includes increasing awareness on the side of the patient and taking deliberate steps to stimulate good feeling. This will ultimately lead to thinking patterns that are healthier and more rational.

Even though recognizing or identifying thoughts does not guarantee wellness, different thinking patterns are altered differently thus bringing about different CBT techniques.

Effective CBT practices also focus on the underlying causes of negative thinking patterns. For example, resistance can occur due to factors even the individual does not recognize or consciously acknowledge. In this case, thorough analysis of the person's relationship history should be done. Social alteration might take longer depending on how long the person is affected by history. CBT becomes the best option for thought alteration because there are different techniques to be applied based on the common cognitive distortions associated with behavior.

Methods of Cognitive Behavioral Therapy

Dialectical behavior therapy

This involves the incorporation of emotional regulation with thinking patterns. It also includes working mindfulness techniques aimed at improving personal relationships. The technique is an active cognitive behavioral therapy, where people are taught how to cope with stress using healthy applications.

Another benefit of dialectical behavioral therapy (DBT), is the ability of the individual to learn the living in the moment pattern. To be less worried about the things of the past or the future and focus intently on the present, while acknowledging past details to help in facilitating decision-making.

It is used basically to treat patients with substance abuse and an eating disorder. DBT has been used recently to treat veterans with post-traumatic stress disorder.

Multimodal therapy

This type of cognitive behavioral therapy is focused on addressing modalities which are heavily interconnected. These modalities include:

Cognition

Imagery

Sensation

Effect

Behavior

Biological consideration

And interpersonal factors.

These seven interconnected modalities are addressed one after the other at different stages of CBT. Multimodal therapy is one of the most sophisticated forms of cognitive behavioral therapy.

Cognition has to do with thinking patterns and thought distortions;

Imagery has to do with the recollection of thoughts and creative visualization;

Sensation has to do with the feeling associated with thoughts and recollection of imagery;

The effect has to do with the effects of particular thought patterns long and short-term;

19

Behavior has to do with a response due to the short or long-term sensation and thought pattern;

Biological consideration involves genetics;

Interpersonal factors involves the interaction of the person with the environment and people, and how history affects present behavior.

Cognitive therapy

Cognitive therapy is focused on identification and change. It identifies a distorted and inaccurate behavioral response, emotional response and thinking patterns. Different considerations are taken to change distorted thinking patterns, emotions, and behaviors.

Rational emotive behavior therapy (REBT)

Using this form of CBT, irrational beliefs and thought patterns are altered using the identification process in cognitive therapy. But in the case of REBT, causal patterns are discovered and dealt with directly. This includes irrational beliefs about self and the environment. Once identified, a set of treatment patterns are being followed to counter the beliefs at first, followed by ways to change the patterns entirely. These stages might take several weeks but very effective in changing distorted thinking patterns.

CBT For Alcohol Abuse Recovery

Sources of negativity – identification

The patient is expected to work directly with the therapist to figure out the various sources for compulsive drinking. Obvious causes of drinking should be written based on the background story, friends, and underlying problems in the office or at home. Also, personal reasons should be considered. Drinking is mostly personal since people drink to conceal pain or to avoid confronting a problem. There must be a clear indication for reasons before a record is taken.

Observe the environmental and social factors surrounding drinking, and you will understand directly from the individual's viewpoint how drinking became relevant to them. Also, daily activities will be observed to identify any source of stress or external negativity that may lead to compulsive drinking.

Mindfulness and emotions

What are the general reasons for consuming alcohol in the social setting? Is there any emotion attached to drinking? List them. What are other unhealthy behaviors observed? Is there any chance drinking also leads to other destructive behavior? If yes, why?

So, allow patients to identify the emotions connected to alcohol consumption. It is easier to introduce positive talk when the negative emotions are identified. To achieve a productive response, patients must be able to relate their actions to what they feel about their life, personally and professionally. Since cognitive behavioral therapy aims to introduce habits that will lead to self-compassion, you should spend more time in the process of emotional assessment, and make sure the individual is well-balanced in the process before you proceed.

Negative thinking patterns - recognizing and reframing

Negative thinking patterns are reframed into positive thinking patterns. At this stage the negative thinking pattern causing alcohol abuse is fully recognized, then suggestions will be made on the positive thinking patterns that will go against the environmental and social influences that led to the abuse.

Positive self-talk is the first and simple option, and it is practiced easily using affirmation. This positive self-talk should be written by patients, in response to the question, "How would you respond when faced with the temptation to drink again?" or "How would you respond to the negative pressure felt that led to your drinking?"

You should ask questions based on real-life situations directly relating to the problem at hand. Positive self-talk has worked wonders in the process of CBT. A patient should have at least three different positive self-talk patterns for the week to take charge of the situation effectively.

The practice – coping patterns

At this stage, the therapist and the patient will work together in creating a goal, consisting of the stage by stage process of handling the addiction or abuse. First of all, since alcohol addiction is often caused by stress or avoidance, the goals should be focused on reducing or managing stress and anxiety personalized to the particular person. Also, triggers for drinking should be considered and ways the person is going to deal with them in a real-life situation. The positive self-talk should be involved in the first stages of the goal.

The goal will bring about the personalize coping mechanisms which will be applied in the real world to deal with temptations or pressure that might lead to negative thinking. Most coping mechanisms involve alternative and yet enjoyable activities, meditation, and self-soothing mechanisms. Alternative activities tend to be effective in dealing with compulsiveness. In alcohol abuse, lack of availability also helps a lot.

Positive self-talk tends to be the backbone of CBT when it comes to thought-reframing. Affirmations can be obtained through suggestions by other people, a therapist or by randomly writing things in a journal that might contribute to the ideas of alternative thought patterns. Once the thinking pattern becomes, effective, positive and productive behavior will be observed. The patient will become more confident and will be eager to take further steps to ensure permanent health.

CBT and alcohol abuse

CBT will help in dealing with alcohol abuse in the following ways:

- Identification of negative thoughts and the sources of these thoughts.

- Actively practice ways to respond to negative thoughts.

- Develop new habits and alternatives that will put down alcohol abuse.

Cognitive behavioral therapy keeps the patient from relapse by providing deeper insight into the root cause of drinking, and counter thinking that will solve the problem.

The person will not only stop drinking, but he or she will also develop new ways of dealing with stress. CBT patterns help in understanding one's emotions and sources of negative thoughts. So, the person will develop better handling of emotions and personal relationships. Instead of becoming destructive or a negative influence, the person will learn how to deal with negativity in the real world and even help others to do the same. Once a patient reaches that stage relapse is very rare. This makes CBT the most effective psychotherapy ever known to man.

The individual will develop stronger willpower.

The person will begin to feel better about themselves, and their environment.

Since they can control their thoughts, there is no need for avoidance. The confidence obtained from the treatment will provide the braveness to face problems instead of avoiding them.

Patients ultimately recognize their fears and sources of distress. The positive alteration of behavior is the biggest impact of CBT.

Instead of spending a lifetime dealing with the same issue, CBT helps you to reach your nearest goals by overcoming doubtful and negative thoughts, feelings, and behavior.

Cognitive Distortions

Cognitive behavioral therapy is focused on dealing with cognitive distortions. These are thoughts that trigger negative emotions. Cognitive distortions push the mind away from reality by enforcing thoughts of the worst-case scenarios. In chronic cognitive distortions, the patient tends to lose touch of reality by believing in an untrue interpretation of information, theories, and thought patterns.

Cognitive distortions include:

Heaven's reward fallacy

This is a belief that every sacrifice done on earth will eventually pay off in the near or far future. Most of these distortion patterns manifest as the expectancy of immediate reward, mostly known as karma. We expect to be rewarded when we do something good, especially when it involves self-sacrifice. There is often a bad feeling and emotional distress when the expected is not achieved. A person with such cognitive distortion does not recognize that not every good thing people do usually lead to good reaction or reward.

Always being right

The need to be right in every situation or circumstance is also a form of cognitive distortion. We believe that being right is definite, we are above mistakes, and nobody should challenge our opinions or actions. There is a constant need for acceptance, and we tend to force the feeling, even if we have to hurt others. People with such distortion tend to despise the feelings of others just to be right. They find it hard to admit of a wrongdoing. They choose to have a distorted relationship than to apologize or admit of a wrongdoing.

Global mislabeling

It is a thought generalization that concludes on the occurrence of one or two situations. We tend to overlook reasons and tend to be negative about things we are not good at executing. For example, it is common for a person having this cognitive distortion to give up on things after a first or second trial. The same case applies when a person you just met say something that doesn't meet your opinion and labeling that person as rude or uncivilized.

In mislabeling, there is always emotions, ego, and exaggerated feeling of inadequacy.

A constant blaming and fault-finding also characterizes it. For example, a man working two jobs and spending more time at the job than at home is abandoning his family—even though in the real sense he is working hard to provide for them.

Fallacy of change

We want everything to be the way we want. Once we start a new relationship, we feel the need to change the other person into exactly what we imagined. Even in a professional world, we tend to see less of the uniqueness in other people and want them to be and act the way we *imagined* our coworkers or employees should act. This distortion also has to do with emotions, where the person's happiness is tied to the way other people behave—how fast they can change or willing to change. They tend to be unhappy when the expected is not met.

Emotional reasoning

When we overly believe our guts, we tend to rely on how we feel in order to judge things. We judge right or wrong by the way we feel about things, without the need to check facts or to confirm with other people. For example, if a woman feels fat, she is definitely fat. This might be a common thinking pattern among women, but the distortion is characterized by extreme reaction towards such thought. And they find it difficult to agree with any other opinion or fact apart from how they feel.

Shoulds

This involves the inbuilt feeling about how things should be done, how people should behave, and how one should respond to similar actions or reactions. There is an extreme feeling, a need to be treated in a certain way, and if that feeling is not met, we tend to get angry. There is a pang of extreme guilt as well if we don't do as we "should" do—and this doesn't have to be a ground-breaking rule. People with such distortions beat themselves up when they are not able to do things according to what they design in their "should do" minds.

Blaming

This distortion is characterized by the need to blame others for whatever goes wrong. Some of the blames are insensible that we suppose to feel inadequate about, but we still tend to get emotional and assign every responsibility to the nearest target. This also includes blaming others by making us act the way we act. It's like hitting the stop sign on the roadside and blaming the person that called you on the phone, even when they don't know that you were driving.

Fallacy of fairness

A constant need for extreme fairness can manifest as cognitive distortion. We all know that life is not fair and more often than we desire, we may experience or witness situations that prove it. People with the fallacy of fairness tend to be extremely unhappy and resentful when experiencing an unfair situation. They want everything to go their way, which is not possible in the real world. They tend to be extremely emotional about situations that depict unfairness.

Control fallacies

It's a cognitive distortion when we think everything that happens to us or the people around us is a result of our or someone else's actions. Some things happen to us due to actions and forces beyond our control and understanding. But it is only faulty to think that such forces control everything we do. Not everything bad or good that happens to you is as a result of your actions. Some are, but not everything is a reaction to your action. Your life quality does not have to do with the people you work with; it doesn't have to do with what someone did. Our actions are connected, but not with a strong bond as we all thought.

Personalization

Again, there is an instance when we feel some things happen because of our actions.

Definitely, many things may happen because of a certain action we took. But it is a distortion to think that we are impacting people with everything we do. Sometimes there is a link between us and the things happening outside; sometimes there isn't any. Most often, people with such distortions believe that some bad things happen because they are too weak to act fast or because they are distracted by other things, even though in reality it isn't their fault, and they don't have a real link with the entire situation.

Catastrophizing

It is a distortion to think that a small mistake can turn everything upside down. For example, if you made a mistake in your speech by starting a sentence differently and then correcting it, a person with such distortion will feel like the whole purpose of the speech is ruined. When you have to work in a team, and you made a mistake somewhere within a given task, and you think that the project is ruined, it means you are catastrophizing. This involves negative thinking, and people with such cognitive distortion tend to see the negative sides of things as bigger than the positive sides, even when reverse is the case.

Jumping to conclusions

We disregard evidence and jump into conclusions. This can happen in favorable and unfavorable conditions, and both can be detrimental to your relationship. Such cognitive distortions often lead to hasty decision-making. More often, the conclusion

40

tends to be negative. There is often no proof that something is not working well, but we tend to ponder and even have sleepless nights. When we jump into conclusions, we tend to think of the negative effects of the conclusion instead of thinking of ways to prove whether we are right or wrong about the conclusion.

Overgeneralization

Overgeneralization is more like jumping into conclusions, but this might be characterized by the use of single evidence to generalize a behavior pattern or result of an action. It also involves beating oneself about not being adequate especially with a shred of slight evidence. This is categorized as distortion when the person concludes that they are no good in all areas when criticized by one person. They tend to despise or avoid other forms of feedback and dwell in the negative emotion due to single evidence, thus building towards a destructive thought pattern.

Polarized thinking

Also known as black and white thinking. This is a form of cognitive distortion that ignores any shades of grey in judgment. They believe something must be either good or bad, and there is no way something could be moderate. There is only failure and success. If they don't obtain a good result in the workplace, they tend to label themselves as failures, even when they have never tried something else. Also, polarized thinking is one form of chronic cognitive distortion because it can lead to depression, and most often it is misdiagnosed for other distortions or disorders.

Filtering

This is a distortion when we ignore all the positive things around us and focus solely on the negative things. Filtering is the subconscious act of feeding the negative thoughts. People with such distortions tend to ignore the good things and good people around them, and instead dwell in the negative part of their day. Sometimes, they find reasons to justify their feelings by using physical stimulations to give them reasons to dwell in negativity. Reverse-filtering is often applied in cognitive behavioral therapy to filter negative thoughts by focusing on negative aspects of life, environment, and people. It is focused on aligning the mind to focus on the abundance in one's environment, and developing a sense of appreciation and acceptance.

Tools and Techniques For CBT

Relaxed breathing

This is a mindfulness technique that involves breathing to achieve total calmness. In the 21st century, relaxed breathing is achieved with the aid of recordings, slide imagery, and videos. Relaxed breathing aims to achieve consistent yet effortless rhythm when breathing. This puts the mind in a position of total balance. The person will become insightful and will develop an effective decision-making ability. There is thought facilitation that will bring about control of intrusive thoughts, therefore having power over the kind of reactions that will take place.

Progressive muscle relaxation

Also termed PMR, is a relaxation technique also in mindfulness but also used in CBT to provide a better form of muscle relaxation. It involves the use of audio guidance and total control of movements of the muscles by series of instructions set in place. The aim is too sooth an unfocused mind. It is more effective when the exercise is carried out in a quiet place than in a noisy place. Apart from soothing the mind, such a technique also helps in calming the nerves, therefore relieving stress. PMR is best practiced when tension due to stress is noticed during CBT diagnosis.

Script thought experiment

Fear and anxiety are best dealt with when the person can understand exactly what is going on. The person is instructed to imagine the worst scenario and its outcome. *They should be allowed to think of themselves in that situation and aftermath.* Mostly, they will realize that the bad situation will not change their lives as much as they thought. Most of the things people are afraid of are not as detrimental or distorting to lives as they imagine. It is normal to be afraid of change, but human nature adapts to change as fast as possible.

Exposure and re-scripting of nightmares

This technique is used to deal with nightmares. Closely related to interoceptive exposure, the nightmare is played out in order to bring similar emotion into play. In every bad emotion, there is another desired emotion. When a person is terrified, there is the desired emotion to feel safe, brave, or happy. Once the primary emotion is identified, the desired emotion is then developed, and a CBT technique to overcome such will be introduced stage by stage. This will help deal with the nightmare and every thought pattern or emotions that contribute to panics.

Interoceptive exposure

Interoceptive exposure is a CBT technique that is issued to treat anxiety and panic attacks. Elicitation of response is the first aim for interoceptive exposure. The feared objects, details, or bodies are reintroduced in the environment through description or physical exposure, just to stimulate the emotions, thought patterns, and beliefs. Also, sensations and avoidance that have to do with panic attacks are activated. Once activated, and the person is still acknowledging he is under supervision, there is a recognition and identification of reason. So, there will be a new understanding of the reasons and thought patterns such panic attacks or anxiety takes place.

Response prevention due to exposure

People with obsessive-compulsive disorder are treated using the exposure and response prevention technique. This is initiated by exposing the patient to situations prompting compulsive behavior. When you consciously expose yourself to such situations, you know that the best you can do is resist the need to take action. Instead of behaving compulsively, write down how you feel in your journal. It is always easy to describe your feelings by writing. Use writing to distract yourself from compulsive actions. Once you understand how the thought patterns bring about such behavior, you will have a better grip on the ways to alternate your thinking.

Cognitive restructuring

There are more cognitive distortions than most people recognize. Whenever you notice an inaccurate and persistent behavior that contradicts the normal, try and find out how the behavior starts. Your aim is to stop feeling bad about things that do not suppose to make you feel bad. Look for reasons why you believed in those things in the first place and why your beliefs don't make sense now.

If you feel the need to blame someone about everything that goes bad in your life, try to find reasons why you need to blame someone. Maybe it is because you need to be respected and you think accepting fault makes you weak.

Counterthought: People love other people who admit they are human; who admit they can make mistakes; who can improve with time; who are confident even when they are not perfect.

Discover distortions

With the list provided in this book, you will easily recognize a new cognitive distortion when you feel it. One characteristic of cognitive distortion is feeling bad without a rational reason. Also, people around you will be distressed and taken aback by your behavior—when your behavior is not normal but still can't find a rational explanation for it. When you feel bad at the end of the day but still repeat the same thing the next day; when you have distressing thoughts without physical triggers. Distortions can also be defined based on a level of vulnerability.

Journaling

Self-CBT involves writing down your thoughts each time you feel that overwhelming and distressing thought. When writing a journal consider the following points:

- The environment the mood or thought starts
- The time
- Sources (you can write down as many sources as you can think of)

- The intensity of the feeling (rate your feeling on the scale of 1-10)
- How you reacted
- How you feel at the moment

By writing and acknowledging these data, you will be conscious of the triggers of negative thinking patterns, and you will be smarter in finding alternative thought patterns in order to avoid distorted emotions.

You will begin to adapt to new situations even as you embrace change.

You will learn the simplest and yet effective coping mechanism relevant to your state of mind.

Journaling is very effective in identifying thought patterns and responsive behaviors. Always keep your journal close and compare your entries from time to time to have a better understanding.

Behavioral experiments

This is a "what if" experiment that focuses on simple alternatives to thinking patterns. It is targeted to stimulate feelings due to different outcomes of projected thoughts. Different thoughts produce different feelings. Behavioral experiments aim to consider more thought patterns and how they affect the feelings of the individual.

This theme goes with negative vs. positive stimulation or motivation. For example, "what if I remove all the support systems, will I be motivated to work towards achieving my goals?" VS. "What if I have all the support systems available, will I still have the motivation to work towards achieving my goals?"

One thought at a time, you are required to record the feelings associated with the thought process. The first side of criticism or lack should be recorded first, then the one for support and kindness.

In comparing the results, you will learn which of the two motivate you to do better, and which one pushes you toward potential negative behavior or thought. Also, it helps in the process of personal growth, where you will choose the best method, using negativity and positivity as a motivation. You will realize that most of the things we feel are just feelings, and you can easily overcome failure by taking needed action.

Thought records

Recording your thoughts will give you a better insight into your weaknesses and strengths. Self-evaluation becomes easy when thinking patterns can be analyzed from outside. Thought recording gives an opportunity for the creation of patterns capable of working against unwanted thoughts.

Recording your thoughts is more like looking for evidence, to evaluate whether your thoughts are running wild or triggered as a result of a physical, present, or past evidence. Future thoughts will be easily evaluated, and you will begin to have more control over the kind of thoughts you will allow to invade your mind.

In the process, you can still look for evidence and reasons why you are not such a bad or horrible person. For example, if your boss didn't see you the minute you wanted to see him, you might think that you are doing bad or you are not valuable enough for the company. But think of the follow-up situation: Your boss actually called you later on, and had a good conversation with you. He even gave you a new task, which clearly indicates that you are valuable after all. In this scenario, the first thought was that you are being ignored by the person you would like to impress. Then come to think of it, you are not being ignored, maybe your boss was busy. But then he was able to squeeze time for you. Now he thinks you are valuable and you are even invited to a house party.

This is a very simple and elementary example, but I want to paint the picture clearly so you can apply this method to alleviate negative thoughts: you should always bring to the picture a second thought against your first distressing and self-despising thoughts. That way you will have better evidence to build your self-confidence.

Do not always think from your point of view. Think of the other person as well. They may have their own issue for behaving the way they do. You don't always have to be the reason things happen badly. It is only logical to acknowledge that other people can be at fault too. It is only logical to have a rational thought about a distressing feeling. That way you will be free of unreasonable thoughts.

Pleasant activity scheduling

One of the most important benefits of having goals is the acknowledgment of purpose. *Activity scheduling* has been introduced to depression patients in cognitive therapy practices. This cognitive behavioral therapy technique has shown a lot of positive effect in warding off depression.

Setting goals keeps your mind away from the present negativities and distressing thoughts, as you look forward to having an eventful, yet fulfilling week ahead.

One of the best methods is to write down your activities for the week at the beginning of each week. For example, on a Sunday, you can list the days starting from Monday to Saturday, then start brainstorming on the fun, fulfilling, and goal-achieving activities you should be doing throughout the week. Record those activities according to convenience. Make sure your goals are realistic and familiar at first.

After the first week, you can always add more challenging goals. This should include physical activities, socializing, and taking the financial step you've been procrastinating about in the past. But in the first week, you should choose things you have done before like visiting a friend, talking to the neighbors, taking a walk, going to the movies, etc. All the activities should be pleasant and not threatening to your confidence. On the other hand, do not schedule activities that will be harmful to your health. Things we do that are harmful to our health tend to just happen, no need of planning them.

If one week is too much, try planning your day the night before. This way you don't have to plan for big events, just little things that give you comfort. Planning to wake up at a certain time to pursue certain activity will give you a head start on how you want your day to go.

In activity scheduling, the aim is to make you feel the effect of purpose; the feeling of accomplishment and to reward yourself whenever you are able to reach a given goal. Your mind and feelings will begin to align with the positivity of the day. Your activities will align toward warding off negative triggers and focusing on things that will motivate you so that you will feel accomplished at the end of the day.

Imagery based exposure

This involves replaying bad imagery on your mind and recording the strong emotions that followed. It doesn't have to be physical recording like journaling, but the purpose of this technique is to help you analyze the situation based on the emotions produced.

Since the brain is capable of recalling the most awful and hurtful situations, this analysis becomes easier when you think of your interaction with people in the workplace or at home. For example, think of the worst thing someone said to you at work recently. Or maybe, the fight you had with your friend or lover—from something the other person said to you that was hurtful to your feelings.

What are the urges associated with your reaction after you are told those things?

What do you feel like doing at the moment? Write your emotions vividly and ponder about them. Once you can put those emotions into mind, the same triggers cannot stimulate the same emotions, not in the same situation. The triggers become less powerful, and the emotions less harmful to your state of mind.

Situation exposure hierarchies

Situation exposure is one of the most effective CBT techniques that focuses directly on the problem at hand. You have to first determine whether you are dealing with social anxiety or depression, then make a list of the things you usually avoid at your critical moments. For example, a person with social anxiety may avoid attending a party, making phone calls, talking to strangers, or even involving in physical activities.

List those things a person with chronic social anxiety will avoid, and then rate those activities on the scale of 1-10 considering how distressing an activity would be to you. For example, if asking a girl out is on the list; consider how distressing it would feel to ask a girl out, and rate the distress on the scale of 1 – 10. Scale 1-5 is below average to average, while 6 -10 is average to severe distress.

Take your time to make such rating, and rearrange them based on the most distressing to the less distressing.

In normal CBT situations, we are advised to deal with a less distressing item, going up the list. In this case, you will need all the support and time to be comfortable with the first situation before jumping to the next. You don't have to rush your way up the ladder. The more time you spend working on your fears and sources of anxiety, the better long-term result you will achieve.

It is not going to be easy. Remember, you are facing difficulty, and you want to become a better person. This is a work that requires effort and consistency.

How To Reframe A Negative Thought

Negative thoughts are easy to adopt, so acting fast against them yields a greater positive impact. Thought-reframing technique is coined by Anderson et al., is bent upon reframing negative thoughts at a first encounter. Whenever you feel negative about something new, try as fast as possible to look for alternative detail that will give a positive feeling. For example, when you enter a room and immediately think you don't like the wall color, you can as well consider the people, the opportunity, the windows, furniture, etc., to have at least one positive feeling that will counter the negative.

The affirmation "Think of the positive things around you." Helps a lot to remember to take such actions.

Negative thought reframing is one of the cognitive behavioral therapy activities that require personal effort. You have to determine to work towards this goal, regardless of the challenges involved.

Creative visualization

This technique involves visualizing the best-case scenario whenever you have a negative feeling. First of all, write down the positive things about your day, and then go over those details to find ways you can use them. It may be a little hard to think of positive things when depressed, but you need to be in a quiet place to create this list.

Start with the things you are thankful for, then proceed to the things without you cannot live. After being able to write at least five things. Sit back and deliberate on how these things affected your life positively. Think of people, good people. Think of the things you have done in the past, good things. Recall how brave you were, and how you are still the same person.

Self-statement technique

This involves writing a statement about self as a form of therapy. Write down counter-thoughts about a negative thought. This technique should be applied regarding persistent negative thoughts about oneself. Negative thoughts about self are distressing especially when they are formed from a lack of physical or mental capacity to be insightful or deal with a certain problem. The thoughts will trigger the feeling of worthlessness. Fortunately these can be countered by a positive thought.

You can start by reciting the following affirmation:

"I am the same person who was strong, and I have experience on my side, so I am better, and I can do even better when given the opportunity."

Or "I have a lot of potentials and I will explore them sooner or later. The difficulty I am passing through is temporary, and I will soon prove myself to the world."

"I am better. I am strong. I am very sophisticated."

Write different forms of thoughts relevant to counter the negative thoughts. This will make it easier to stay above the negative thought and feelings and to dwell in the hopes and even to be determined to take actions that will confirm your self-confidence.

Successive Approximation Technique

Split your goal into smaller tasks in order to make them achievable. You don't need to be passing through depression or anxiety to be overwhelmed by large goals. No one would be comfortable taking up big tasks with the hope of accomplishing them in the next six months. So instead of making a long term and bigger goals, break your goals into smaller pieces and apply them on a daily basis. Smaller goals are achievable, and you will always go back home with your reward of satisfaction.

Having optimal mental health can be a large goal, but if you break them into pieces, you won't have to suffer *anxiety* from the need to overcome your anxiety. If you want to build a house start by putting together materials first, you don't have to start building immediately. You can always start with the foundation and make progress.

Self-improvement starts with taking a step to becoming better at doing something you already know and then moving to something a little bit challenging, a step at a time. Within a month or two, you will look back and will realize how far up you are on the ladder.

Meditation and mindfulness

Meditation is one of the effective methods of accumulating positive thoughts. Mindfulness meditation, on the other hand, is one of the holistic ways to deal with addiction, anxiety, and depression. The first rule of disengagement from persistent unwanted thoughts is meditation. It provides a stronghold, where you will develop a particular comfort, dwelling in a particular environment where your thoughts control everything. You get rid of obsessive thoughts and only dwell in thoughts you prefer. In mindfulness meditation, you choose your thoughts and live in it.

The acceptance technique

This technique is based on controlling your thought response to negative situations, especially to those situations that cause direct disappointments. It is aimed at changing the way individuals deal with disappointments.

A broken relationship can generally change your mood and may bring about persistent thought patterns making you feel like a total failure.

Thoughts such as "I have tried a lot, but I still can't maintain a reasonable relationship.", "What's the point of trying? What is the point of looking good? Will I stop going to the gym? I will eat junk food and get fat since nobody cares."

Such thoughts can be hard to dismiss amidst such emotional disappointments. The best way to overcome such thought patterns is by handling your emotions from outside.

Instead of cutting down on healthy activities and giving up on looking good, you can resort to more rigorous activities to shed the emotions. You are not to avoid negative emotions, but you have to deal with them in such a way they don't have a negative effect on your mental and physical health. Feel everything you have to feel. Cry for some time if that is what you want. But consider the things you still have control over, such as yourself, your activities, and your career. Find a better replacement and fill up the hole created by the breakup. Use what you have in control to control all your negative emotions—don't allow yourself to be out of control.

This technique will take time and a bit of courage. Do not resort to avoidance techniques like drinking and isolation. You are allowed to feel the pain, and still, dare to be the boss where you have control. If you cannot handle the emotions alone, talk to someone—that someone does not have to be a professional. Talk to a friend or family member you trust, not to look for advice but to talk about your feelings.

Talking alone reduces the strength of distress. The first step is talking about it, and you will begin to have the courage to take further bold steps in dealing with every negative feeling. The activities are very important, hence cognitive behavioral therapy. Keep a record of your feelings and the lessons obtained from your recent distress, that way you will have a definite goal to become a better person and thrive efficiently.

Start positive

Your initial thought will always determine your experience. The positive-start technique is focused on encouraging individuals to have a positive consciousness about things around them. For example, upon facing a challenging situation, you can start with "oh well, another opportunity to prove myself." Instead of "ugh another challenge/disappointment."

Consciously develop a positive first approach even to the most unpleasant situations. That way once you begin positive, everything will be easier, and you will be less affected by negativity that may come after that.

This technique is best applied in the morning. Leaving your bed, you should think "oh another beautiful morning!", "It's time to start my day and reach my target goal." "Time to get a little bit bigger.". Your day should be treated as an opportunity instead of a burden.

Solution-based technique

Before meeting a therapist experiment your capability of figuring out the problem. Use the ideas you have about what is bothering you and write down some suggestions on what you would do to feel better. Go over the suggestions and choose the ones more relevant to your activities.

You will discover that there are healthy ways to deal with problems apart from avoidance. You don't have to find a concrete solution, just some simple ways to feel better and feel like an improved person. Let all your solutions be action-based to experience a fast positive effect.

Conclusion

The self-help materials provided in this book are to help you recognize and understand the concept of cognitive behavioral therapy. The most important aspect of CBT is not the vast techniques but the ability to set reasonable goals to climb the ladder of improvement. Distortions such as anger, panic attacks, eating disorders, addictions, depressions, phobias, and anxiety can be treated using CBT. But note you cannot solve every problem at once. Take one issue at a time and set realistic goals. Your goals have to be specified to the improvement you desire.

There is a window for self-exploration in the process of CBT. A therapist can only instruct you on the things you should be doing. Everything is focused and structured. All you need to do is spend the time to analyze your thought patterns and feelings. Once you identify the source of the problem, the self-analysis should begin.

There is an opportunity for learning about behavior and emotional distress. The coping skills learned in CBT will build the individual to become stronger emotionally and to deal with problems efficiently.

Your present thoughts and feelings are factors to be considered, and how to achieve permanent change.

BOOKS BY THE SAME AUTHOR

- <u>Ketogenic Diet for Beginners: Simple Keto Recipes and Diet Plan to Lose Fat, Heal Your Body, and Boost Energy</u>
- <u>How to Reverse Fibromyalgia Cookbook: Recipes and Meal Plan to Relieve Symptoms and Treat Root Cause</u>
- <u>CBD Hemp Oil Beginners Guide: The Healing Benefits of Cannabidiol Essential Oil</u>
- <u>How to Reverse Hashimoto's Thyroiditis: Eliminate Root Cause and Heal Hypothyroidism Symptoms Naturally</u>
- <u>Paleo Diet Cookbook: Nutritional Recipes to Boost Health and Prevent Toxicity</u>

- <u>Adrenal Fatigue Solution: Powerful Methods to Boost Your Energy, Improve Metabolism, And Stimulate Your Hormones</u>

www.ingramcontent.com/pod-product-compliance
Lightning Source LLC
Chambersburg PA
CBHW051219250726
48655CB00006B/2501